# 7 SMART STEPS OF WEALTH MANAGEMENT

**Kaushik Sen**

**First published in 2020 by**


**Becomeshakespeare.com**
One Point Six Technologies Pvt. Ltd.
119-123, 1st floor, Building No. J2, Wadala East,
Wadala Truck Terminal, Mumbai, Maharashtra 400037, India
T: +91 8080226699







ISBN 978-93-90463-52-7

# About the Author

Kaushik Sen, has been working in the financial markets since 1995. He completed his MBA Degree, with finance as specialisation, in first class, from Pune University. He has worked as Area Manager at Bonanza Portfoilio Limited ( A stock broking firm ) for a brief period. He has also studied technical analysis and fundamental analysis and has been stock market Analyst and was also a member of Association of Technical Market Analysts (ATMA).

*Dedicated to my Family Members and Clients*

# Disclaimer

Please note that the facts and figures mentioned in the book are based on the latest information available at the time of publishing. Since they could change with time, readers should verify the information before taking any financial decision.

Also note that not all investments covered in  this book maybe suitable for every investor. Investment needs depend totally on individual situations and this book in no way recommends one investment option over the other. Readers are requested to make their own investigations and seek appropriate professional advice before opting for any of the investment options mentioned.

While due care has been taken in compiling the information for the book, we do not guarantee that the content, recommendations and analysis are complete and accurate. The author and publisher do not accept any responsibility or liability, whatsoever, for any error, omission, opinion or misrepresentation of information, however it may have occurred, and disclaim any liability to any person or group for the consequences of any decisions based on the contents of this book.

# Acknowledgements

I wish to express my gratitude to all the people who have supported me in my career.

I would like to thank my clients, team members, for supporting and motivating me to continue my good work, and acquire my experiences, needed to write this book.

Also I would like to thank my teachers and faculties, who taught me in my schools and colleges, for giving me such high level of knowledge and understanding, to be able to pen down my thoughts.

This book is reflection of my experiences, gained while working in the financial markets since 1995. And this could not have been possible without the support of my clients and distributors.

# Contents


| | | |
|---|---|---|
| **Introduction** | | **13** |
| 1. | **Meaning of Real Wealth** | **15** |
| 2. | **Net Worth and Net Value** | **18** |
| 3. | **Time Value of Money** | **21** |
| 4. | **Cash** | **23** |
| 5. | **Debt** | **25** |
| 6. | **Equity** | **44** |
| 7. | **Commodity** | **53** |
| 8. | **Life Insurance** | **57** |
| 9. | **Health Insurance** | **62** |
| 10. | **Real Estate** | **65** |
| 11. | **Smart Step 1: Do proper Financial Planning and Goal Setting** | **67** |
| 12. | **Smart Step 2: Maintain Necessary Liquidity** | **69** |
| 13. | **Smart Step 3: Have Proper Risk Coverage** | **70** |
| 14. | **Smart Step 4: Plan for Long Term** | **72** |
| 15. | **Smart Step 5: Don't follow Past Performance Track blindly** | **73** |

16.    **Smart Step 6: Don't follow others blindly**    75

17.    **Smart Step 7: Always review the portfolio periodically**    77

18.    **Common Mistakes that common investors should avoid**    78

**Conclusion**    82

# Introduction

In 1995, just after completing my class 12, I had joined the financial industry by taking up agency of Life Insurance Corporation of India. My sole objective at that time was to gain some experience, while continuing my studies. Never had I imagined at that time, that I would find my full time profession in the financial markets.

While working in the financial markets, I had the opportunity to meet and interact with lot of clients. What I understood was that there were lot of gaps in the knowledge and awareness level of clients. If the clients don't understand the financial products well, how can they decide what is best for them.

So this book is written in simple language to educate the clients, so that they can take the correct decisions. I have ensured that not much technical jargons are used in this book, so that the readers can understand easily.

Financial advisors are there to advise clients, but without basic understanding level among clients, there is huge chance of mis-communication and mis-selling.

What I have seen, during these long 24 years, majority of clients, pose to understand a lot, without even knowing the basics, or they leave the entire decision to the financial advisors. This should not be the case. Clients should have the basic awareness. Financial advisers are supposed to give various options and explain the technicalities, and clients are supposed to chose from the options.

So I have written this book to make the clients more educated and aware about the Indian financial markets and various investment options.

# CHAPTER 1

# Meaning of Real Wealth

What is real wealth?

Is wealth visible?

How to determine who is wealthy?

Does wealth mean only money?

Why do we need wealth?

I was flying from Mumbai to Delhi. I had tickets for the economy class. While going to my seat, every-time I have to cross the front row seats, which comprise the business class. And every-time I keep wondering who are these people sitting in the front row. Are they very rich and wealthy! Maybe Yes. Maybe No. How to decide! If the persons had huge liability, much more than me, are they wealthier than me! If they are employees of some organisation, and the tickets are sponsored by the company, are they wealthier than me! Thus it can be said that real wealth is not always visible. A visible rich lifestyle does not always depict real wealth.

Wealth maybe defined as an abundance of valuable possessions or money.

Wealth refers to the value of everything a person or family owns. This includes tangible items such as jewellery, housing, cars, and other personal property. Financial assets such as stocks and bonds, which can be traded for cash, also contribute to wealth. Wealth is measured as "net assets", that is how much asset one owns, minus "net debt', that is, how much debt one owes.

Wealth is a great amount of money, property, possessions, or ideas. An example of wealth maybe the money, property, and business of Mr. Mukesh Ambani.

There maybe 4 types of wealth:

- Financial Wealth  (Money & Asset)
- Social Wealth (Status)
- Time Wealth (Freedom)
- Physical Wealth (Health)

But in this entire book, by wealth, we shall be referring to only Financial Wealth, and we shall be dealing with ways to create and enhance Financial Wealth.

Building financial wealth is important for a healthy retirement. Wealth matters because it can enable one to continue living even when there is no source of income.

Building wealth is important for creating a legacy. Wealth matters because it is only the wealth that can be transferred to the next generation.

Building wealth is important for having freedom. Wealth matters because it allows spending time and leisure as per choice, rather than working to earn more money or worrying about how to earn more money.

Real wealth gives the ability to enjoy available resources for self well being and also to contribute to others' well-being. It also helps to create a kind of self-possession. It might not always be physically visible.

# CHAPTER 2

# Net Worth and Net Value

One of my *rich* neighbour, lives in a big 2000 square feet flat, in a posh locality of South Kolkata. He works in a big corporate house and draws a monthly salary of Rupees 5 Lakhs. He has 3 cars including one BMW. Coincidentally, his flats and the cars are taken on bank loan.

One of my *poor* friends, lives in a small house in the suburbs of Kolkata, having 5 Kattah land adjoining to his house. He works in a government department, earns a meagre monthly salary of Rupees 20 thousand. He does not have any car also. He goes to the office regularly on his cycle. But, coincidentally he does not have any bank loan or liability.

Now, who is rich or poor?

Who is wealthier?

Who has more net worth?

Net worth refers to everything one owns (assets) minus what one owes in debts (liabilities). Assets include cash and investments, home and other real estate, cars, jewellery, or anything else of value. Liabilities include all loans.

One can calculate net worth by subtracting all liabilities (debts) from all assets.

We can say that only visible assets might not give the correct idea of the wealth of a person. The net worth of a person can to a certain extent, help in calculating the wealth of a person.

Now how is "Value" different from "Worth"?

Are they both the same?

Which is more important, value or worth, for wealth creation?

One of my friends, Rajsekhar bought a brand-new BMW car paying Rs. 60 Lakhs.

Another friend of mine, Samuel bought a brand new flat in a posh locality paying Rs. 60 Lakhs.

As per the books of account, both the purchases create the same net worth. But does it create the same net value?

After 5 years, what can be the value of the 2 assets? In an ideal scenario, the value of the flat would have appreciated. And obviously, the value of the car would have depreciated. At the time of purchase, the net worth of both the assets maybe the same, but down the years, the net value of both the assets should not remain the same.

So we can say that net worth and net value are not the same. Now, which of the above two assets will help to make a person wealthy? Obviously, which will add "value" in the coming years.

So we can say that net value is more important than net worth for purpose of wealth creation. We need to focus on creating "future value" than creating "present worth", to be able to create more wealth.

# CHAPTER 3

# Time Value of Money

Suppose I plan to invest Rupees 1 Lakh in some investment scheme. If I am supposed to get back Rupees 2 Lakh in two schemes, after 10 Years in one of the schemes, and after 15 years in another scheme, are the returns the same? Which one is better? Obviously, if the maturity returns are equal, the earlier the maturity the better it is. So the first scheme will be better for investment. And this is the time value of money.

The time value of money (TVM) is the concept that money you have now is worth more than the identical sum in the future due to its potential earning capacity. The core principle of finance holds that provided money can earn interest, any amount of money is worth more the sooner it is received. TVM is also sometimes referred to as present discounted value.

The time value of money is based on the idea that people would rather have money today than in the future.

Given that money can earn compound interest, it is more valuable in the present rather than the future.

The formula for computing time value of money considers the payment now, the future value, the interest rate, and the time frame.

In general, the most fundamental TVM formula takes into account the following variables:

- FV = Future value of money
- PV = Present value of money
- R = Interest rate
- T = Number of years

Based on the above variables, the formula for TVM are as below:

$$FV = PV \times [\,1 + (R/100)\,\char94\,T]$$

$$PV = FV / [\,1 + (R/100)\,\char94\,T\,]$$

# CHAPTER 4

# Cash

What is Cash?

Cash is legal tender, currency or coins, that can be used to exchange for goods, debt or services.

Cash can be told to be the oxygen of life. Without cash, life cannot go on. Cash gives us the purchasing power. If we go to some shop or establishment, and we want to take some goods or services, we need to pay in cash for it.

Cash helps in taking care of our present requirements. But it does not give us any future value appreciation.

Say I have Rupees 100/- currency note with me. Maybe I can buy 1 Litre mustard oil currently with it. But if I keep the note with me, say for 5 years, and then go to buy mustard oil with that note, maybe I will get 0.5 Litre mustard oil with it.

Thus we can say Cash depreciates with time, if not utilised properly.

So,cash should be part of our assets and wealth. It should be sufficient to take care of our immediate demands and requirements. But it should not be in excess, as idle cash can never grow.

# CHAPTER 5

# Debt

What is Debt?

Debt is a sum of money that is owed or due.

Debt is what someone owes to someone else. Usually, debt is in the form of money, but it can also be items, services, favours or other things. Thus if one makes an agreement to give something to someone else, it can be said that he or she owes a debt.

But what has a debt to do with wealth creation?

By debt, we would hereby refer to debt products, wherein individuals and institutions can invest.

Debt products in Indian markets constitute of:

- Government bonds
- Bank fixed deposits
- Company fixed deposits
- Postal savings
- Debt mutual funds

- Conventional life insurance policies (To be discussed in the life insurance chapter)

Investment in all debt products are free from any sort of market risks and volatility.

Debt products give security and stability, but will never give very high returns. Some debt products which carry a sovereign guarantee, are highly secure. Whereas some debt products like debt mutual funds might have certain risks associated with them.

## Government Bonds

These are bonds issued by the government. They carry a sovereign guarantee.

All the interest and principal payments are guaranteed by the government of India. Therefore, one doesn't have to worry about any default. Government bonds are the safest investment one can make in India, even safer than the bank fixed deposits.

There are two ways to make money by investing in bonds. The first is to hold those bonds upto maturity date and collect all interest payments payable during the entire holding period. Bond interest is usually paid twice a year. The second way to profit from bonds is to sell them at a price that's higher than the purchase price.

Investors buy bonds because they provide a predictable income source. If the bonds are held till maturity, bond holders get back the entire principal, so bonds are a way to preserve capital while investing.

Most bonds pay a fixed interest rate. So if interest rates in general fall, the older bond's interest rates become more attractive, and so the price of the bonds goes up. Likewise, if interest rates rise, people will no longer prefer the lower fixed interest rate paid by the older bond, and hence their price will fall.

Examples of Govt Bonds:

- 7.75% GOI Savings Bond
- Sovereign Gold Bond (SGB)
- Capital Gains Bonds by NHAI & REC
- Indian Railways Finance Corporation (IRFC) Tax-free bonds.

## Bank Fixed Deposits

A bank fixed deposit (FD) is a financial instrument provided by principal banks, regulated by the Reserve Bank of India. It provides investors a higher rate of interest than a regular savings account, until the given maturity date.

Post Covid-19 Crisis, interest on bank fixed deposits in India have fallen drastically and is expected to fall further.

Currently, interest rates offered by the State Bank of India on fixed deposits range from 4.50% to 6.10% depending on tenor. For senior citizens, interest rates are 0.5% extra.

It is to be noted that in India, the maximum official permissible tenor of fixed deposits can be 10 Years, though most banks don't want to offer fixed deposits of tenor higher than 5 years.

Interest payable on fixed deposits are taxable as per the current income tax slab.

## Company Fixed Deposits

The deposit placed by investors with companies for a fixed term carrying a prescribed rate of interest is called a company fixed deposit. Fixed deposits thus mobilised are governed by the companies act under section 58A. These deposits are unsecured, i.e., if the company defaults, the investor cannot sell the documents to recover his capital, thus making them a risky investment option.

As the risk involved in company fixed deposits are much more as compared to bank fixed deposits, the interest rates are generally higher. Interest payable on company fixed deposits are taxable as per tax slab.

If a company fixed deposit has a rating of AAA, it means that it is a safe and secure investment. However, one needs to tread with caution if the rating is lower as there could be numerous risks involved.

But with the recent DHFL or ILFS fiasco, one needs to be very careful while investing in Company Fixed Deposits, even if it has a stable rating. It might take a single day, for ratings to change. With so much volatility and uncertainty in the current market scenario, a company's rating might get changed from 'stable' to 'unstable' in a very short span of time.

## Postal Savings

Postal Savings are very secure as it carries a sovereign guarantee.

- Post Office Time Deposit Account (TD)

    Minimum Rupees 1000/- and in multiple of Rupees 100 /-. No maximum limit.

    Interest is payable annually but calculated quarterly.

    Normally TD Accounts can be for upto 5 Years. But TD account can be extended by giving an application in the accounts office.

    Interest rates from 01.04.2020 to 30.06.2020 are as follows:

    | Period | Rate |
    | --- | --- |
    | 1yr.A/c | 5.5% |
    | 2yr.A/c | 5.5% |
    | 3yr.A/c | 5.5% |
    | 5yr.A/c | 6.7 % |

Interest shall be payable annually, No additional interest shall be payable on the amount of interest that has become due for payment but not withdrawn by the account holder.

Premature encashment is not allowed before the expiry of 6 months. If closed between 6 months to 12 months from the date of opening, Post Office saving accounts interest rate will be payable.

The investment under 5 Years TD qualifies for the benefit of Section 80C of the Income Tax Act, 1961 from 1.4.2007.

Interest payable on TD is taxable as per tax slab.

- Post Office Monthly Income Scheme (MIS)

  From 01.04.2020, interest rates on MIS are 6.6 % per annum payable monthly.

  The maximum investment limit is Rupees 4.5 Lakhs in a single account and Rupees 9 lakh in a joint account

  An individual can invest a maximum of Rupees 4.5 Lakhs in MIS (including his share in joint accounts)

  The maturity period is 5 years w.e.f. 01.12.2011.

  Can be prematurely en-cashed after one year but before 3 years at the discount of 2% of the deposit and after 3 years at the discount of 1% of the deposit. (Discount means deduction from the deposit.)

Interest payable on MIS is taxable as per tax slab.

- Senior Citizens Savings Scheme ( SCSS )

From 01.04.2020, interest rates on SCSS are 7.4% per annum, payable from the date of deposit of 31st March/30th September /31st December in the first instance & thereafter, interest shall be payable on 31st March, 30th June, 30th September, and 31st December.

An individual of the age of 60 years or more may open the account.

An individual of the age of 55 years or more but less than 60 years who has retired on superannuation or under VRS can also open an account subject to the condition that the account is opened within one month of receipt of retirement benefits and the amount should not exceed the amount of retirement benefits.

The maturity period is 5 years.

Premature closure is allowed, as per the following terms:

> If closed before 1 year, no interest will be payable, if paid already will be recovered.

> after 1 year, 1.5% of the deposit to be deducted.

> after 2 years 1% of the deposit to be deducted.

After maturity, the account can be extended for a further three years within one year of maturity by giving application in the prescribed format. In such cases, the account can be closed at any time after the expiry of one year of extension without any deduction.

Interest payable on SCSS is taxable as per tax slab.

TDS is deducted at source on interest if the interest amount is more than Rupees 50,000/- per annum.

- Public Provident Fund ( PPF )

From 01.04.2020, interest rates on PPF are 7.1 % per annum (compounded yearly).

The maturity period is 15 years but the same can be extended within one year of maturity for further 5 years and so on.

Premature closure can be allowed after 5 years from the end of the year in which the account was opened subject to the following conditions:

> In case of life-threatening disease of the account holder, spouse, or dependent children.

- ➤ In case of higher education of account holder or dependent children.

- ➤ In case of change of resident status of the account holder.

- ➤ 1% interest will be deducted from the date of account opening, in case of premature withdrawal.

Interest payable on PPF is completely tax-free.

A loan can be taken after the expiry of one year from the end of the year in which the initial subscription was made but before the expiry of five years from the end of the year in which the initial subscription was made.

No attachment possible under court decree order.

- • National Savings Certificates (NSC - VIII Issue)

From 01.04.2020, interest rates on NSC is 6.8% compounded annually but payable at maturity.

Rupees 1000/- grows to Rupees 1389.49 after 5 years.

The maturity period is 5 years.

Interest earned on NSC is taxable as per tax slab.

- Kisan Vikas Patra (KVP)

  From 01.04.2020, interest rates on KVP are 6.9 % compounded annually.

  Amount invested doubles in 124 months (10 years & 4 months).

  Interest earned on KVP is taxable as per tax slab.

- Sukanya Samriddhi Account

  Rate of interest is 7.6% per annum (with effect from 01-04-2020), calculated on yearly basis, yearly compounded.

  Minimum Rupees 250/- and Maximum Rupees 1.5 Lakhs can be deposited in a financial year. Subsequent deposit can be made in multiples of Rupees 50/-. Deposits can be made in lump-sum. And there is no limit on the number of deposits either in a month or in a financial year.

  A legal guardian/natural guardian can open an account in the name of a girl child.

  A guardian can open only one account in the name of one girl child and a maximum of two accounts in the name of two different girl children.

  The account can be opened up to the age of 10 years only from the date of birth.

If minimum Rupees 250/- is not deposited in a financial year, the account will become discontinued and can be revived with a penalty of Rupees 50/- per year with the minimum amount required for deposit for that year.

Deposits may be made in the account till the completion of a period of fifteen years from the date of opening of the account.

Partial withdrawal, maximum up to 50% of balance standing at the end of the preceding financial year can be taken after the account holder's attaining age of 18 years.

The account can be closed after the completion of 21 years.

Normal premature closure will be allowed after completion of 18 years on the occasion of marriage (1 month before and 3 months from the date of marriage).

Investments made in the SSY scheme are eligible for deductions under Section 80C, subject to a maximum cap of Rupees 1.5 Lakhs. The interest that accrues against this account which gets compounded annually is also exempt from tax. The proceeds received upon maturity/withdrawal are also exempt from income tax.

7 Smart Steps Of Wealth Management

| Scheme | Interest Rate | Minimum Investment | Maximum Investment | Eligibility | Tax Implications |
|---|---|---|---|---|---|
| Post Office Time Deposit Account (TD) | First year – 6.9% p.a. Second year – 6.9% p.a. Third Year – 6.9% p.a. Fourth Year – 7.7% p.a. | Rs 200 | No limit | Individual. | Interest earned is taxable and Tax benefits up to 5 years under section 80C on deposits. |
| Post Office Monthly Income Scheme Account (MIS) | 7.6% p.a. payable monthly | Rs 1,500 | For single account holder – Rs 4.5 lakh. For joint account holder – Rs 9 lakh. | Individual. | Interest earned is taxable and no deduction under Sec 80C for deposits made. |
| Senior Citizen Savings Scheme (SCSS) | 8.6% p.a. (Compounded annually) | Rs 1,000 | Maximum deposit over the lifetime allowed is Rs 15 lakh. | Individual of age> 60 years or age >55 years who have opted for VRS or superannuation. | – Tax benefit under section 80C for deposits – TDS to be deducted on interest earned for more than Rs 50,000 p.a. |

| Scheme | Interest Rate | Minimum Investment | Maximum Investment | Eligibility | Tax Implications |
|---|---|---|---|---|---|
| 15-year Public Provident Fund Account (PPF) | 7.9% p.a. (Compounded annually) | Rs 500 per financial year | Rs 1.5 lakh per financial year | Individual | Tax rebate under section 80C for deposits (maximum Rs 1.5 lakh p.a.) |
| National Savings Certificates (NSC) | 7.9% p.a. (Compounded annually) | Rs 100 | No limit | Individual | Tax rebate under section 80C for deposits (maximum Rs 1.5 lakh p.a.) |
| Kisan Vikas Patra (KVP) | 7.6% p.a. (Compounded annually) | Rs 1,000 | No limit | Individual (Adult) | Interest earned is taxable. |
| Sukanya Samriddhi Account | 8.4% p.a. (Compounded annually) | Rs 1,000 per financial year | Rs 1.5 lakh per financial year | Girl Child – up to 10 years from birth and one additional year of grace. | Investment (up to Rs 1.5 lakh exempt under Section 80C), and Total amount received on maturity is tax-free. |

## Debt Mutual Funds

Debt funds are mutual funds that invest in fixed income securities like bonds and treasury bills. Gilt fund, monthly income plans (MIPs), short term plans (STPs), liquid funds, and fixed maturity plans (FMPs) are some of the investment options in debt funds.

Investments in debt funds are safe because they do not have exposure to volatile assets such as equities.

Exception: When interest rates are rising, long-term debt funds can give negative returns. As in 2009, rising interest rates caused bond prices to slide.

What are the types of debt mutual funds?

- Income Funds— Income funds are mutual funds, ETFs, or any other type of fund that seeks to generate an income stream for shareholders by investing in securities that offer dividends or interest payments.

- Dynamic Bond Funds—Dynamic bond funds are a class of debt mutual funds that alter allocations between short-term and long-term bonds. This strategy helps in taking advantage of fluctuating interest rates.

- Liquid Funds—Liquid funds have high liquidity. They are open-ended income schemes that invest in debt and money market instruments such as government securities, treasury bills, and call money among others. These instruments have a maximum maturity period of 91 days and are considered safe because they mitigate interest rate volatility risk.

- Credit Opportunities Funds—Credit opportunity funds are the debt funds that invest in corporate bonds and debentures of credit rating below

AAA. That is, they invest in low-rated securities with strong fundamentals which are expected to see rating upgrades in the future, benefiting the portfolio and investors.

- Ultra Short-Term Debt Funds—Ultra short duration funds are debt funds that lend to companies for a period of 3 to 6 months. Although these are low-risk funds owing to their low lending duration, they are slightly above liquid funds in the risk spectrum but still one of the lowest risk categories of Schemes to invest in.

- Short-Term Debt Funds— Short term funds are debt funds that lend to companies for a period of 1 to 3 years. These funds mostly take exposure only in quality companies that have a proven record of repaying their loans on time as well as have sufficient cash flows from their business operations to justify the borrowing.

- Gilt Funds—Gilt funds are debt funds that invest primarily in government securities. These funds have no risk of non-payment of interest or principal amount but get affected by interest rate movements as the government borrowing typically happens to be for a longer duration.

- Fixed Maturity Plans—Fixed maturity plans are close-ended debt funds, meaning investments can be made only during the time of a new fund offer. It comes with a fixed maturity period and invests across debt instruments such as high rated securities and corporate bonds. FMPs are ideal for those investors, who need returns higher than a regular FD but can accept the frequent NAV fluctuations. Compared to equity funds, FMPs are low risk-low return investments. Due to the restricted liquidity, investors who are ready to park their money for the NFO tenure can invest in this scheme.

Long term capital gains upto Rupees 1 Lakh is totally tax-free. The minimum holding period for short term capital gains in debt funds is 3 years. Short-term capital gains (if the units are sold before three years) in debt mutual funds are taxed as per the applicable tax rate of the investor.

Investing in debt funds carries various types of risk. These risks include credit risk, interest rate risk, inflation risk, reinvestment risk, etc. But the key risks which need to be considered before investing in debt funds are credit risk and interest rate risk.

## Credit Risk (Default Risk):

The chances that a borrower might not repay the interest or principle on the committed date is considered as credit risk or default risk. Credit risk is measured by "Credit ratings". Credit rating agencies like CRISIL, ICRA, CARE, etc. rate the issuer of the bond on their ability to repay by assessing their overall financial health.

As credit risk increases, the expectation on return also goes up. If a specific debt fund claims to generate very high returns, the first thing that should be checked is the credit risk of the portfolio.

Credit ratings can change over a period of time. The performance of companies is measured and the risk assessment is done at periodic intervals. The risk that a fund manager is worried about is not the risk of default but the possible downgrade in the credit rating of the debt paper. If a debt paper gets downgraded, the market price of such an instrument also comes down which affects the portfolio directly. On the other hand, if the credit rate gets upgraded the fund would be benefited by an increase in its fund value.

- **Real-Life Example:**

  Recently in April 2020, Franklin Templeton Mutual Fund had decided to wind up six debt mutual fund schemes. Investors in these schemes was not able to buy or sell these schemes anymore. No SIP/STP/SWP would work on these schemes.

  The six schemes were: Franklin India Low Duration Fund, Franklin India Dynamic Accrual Fund, Franklin India Credit Risk Fund, Franklin India Short Term Income Plan, Franklin India Ultra Short Bond Fund, and Franklin India Income Opportunities Fund. These schemes managed assets worth Rupees 26,000 Crore.

"Significantly reduced liquidity in the Indian bond markets for most debt securities and unprecedented levels of redemptions following the Covid-19 outbreak and lockdown have compelled us to take this decision," said Sanjay Sapre, president, Franklin Templeton India.

The company was not able to sell its investments because there were no takers in the market. The uncertain situation in the economy and the market had made investors extremely risk-averse. They wanted to play it safe and did not want to buy lower-rated and unrated papers. The fund was not able to sell investments to meet the redemption pressure.

So, one was not able to sell his or her investments. One will have to wait for the fund house to sell its assets and pay the money back. The basic idea behind the decision was  to avoid distress sale to meet redemption proceeds. If the liquidity in the debt market improves, the fund house would be able to sell its assets and pay back the money.

## Interest Rate Risk:

The market price of the bond and interest rates carry an opposite relationship. Whenever interest rates in the market go up, the market prices of bonds come down.

- Example:

  A bond presently available in the market carries a face value of Rupees 100 /- offers 8% coupon rate with the leftover maturity of 3 years.

  The cash flow would be Rupees 8 /- interest for the next 3 years and Rupees 100 /- principal repayment at the end of the third year.

  The current interest rate offered in the market is 9%.

  If the bondholder with 8% coupon rate decides to sell his bond, he might have to sell the bond at a discount on face value. The selling price of the bond would be around Rupees 97.47, which is lesser than the face value.

  Thus the thumb rule is "When the interest rate in the market rises, the market price of the bond comes down & vice-versa"

# CHAPTER 6

# Equity

What is Equity?

Equity can be defined as the value of the shares issued by a company. To put it simply, equities are stocks or shares of a company. A stock or a share refers to the individual blocks that make up the equity of a company. Anybody who holds a stock/share of a company owns a piece of that company. So equity can also be termed as part-ownership of the company.

Investing in equity is the most exciting way to create wealth. Equity investment requires a strong heart as risk factors are associated with it. The investment amount can get doubled in no time if invested in good stocks. Also, the investment amount can become zero if invested in the wrong stocks. Also, patience is required to create wealth from equities.

Equity Investment can be done in 3 ways:

- Direct Equity

- Equity Mutual Funds

- Unit Linked Insurance Plans - ULIPs (To be discussed in Life Insurance Chapter )

## Direct Equity Investment

Herein one directly invests in the stock markets. Equity Investment can be broadly classified into the following categories:

- Primary Market Investment
- Secondary Market Investment

## Primary Market Investment

The primary market is where securities are created, while the secondary market is where those securities are traded by investors. In the primary market, companies sell new stocks and bonds to the public for the first time, in form of initial public offering (IPO).

There are two ways retail investors can buy securities through the primary market:

- Initial Public Offering (IPO):

  An initial public offering or IPO is when a company makes shares available to the public, for the first time.

- Rights Issue:

  An issue of shares offered at a special price by a company to its existing shareholders in proportion to their holding of old shares.

  Companies most commonly issue the rights offering to raise additional capital. A company may need extra capital to meet its current financial obligations. Troubled companies typically use rights issues to pay down debt, especially when they are unable to borrow more money.

For example, a 1:4 rights issue means an existing investor can buy one extra share for every four shares already held by him/her. Usually, the price at which the new shares are issued by way of the rights issue is less than the prevailing market price of the stock, i.e. the shares are offered at a discount.

## Secondary Market Investment

The secondary market is where investors buy and sell securities they already own. It is what most people typically think of as the "Stock Market," though stocks are also sold on the primary market when they are first issued.

Trading in the stock markets has one sole objective, Buy at a low price and sell at a higher price, to generate some profit. But for that one requires a lot of knowledge and research.

We can divide stock market transactions mainly into 3 categories:

- Intraday Trading –

  Herein, the investor or trader buys and sells stocks on the same day itself. In this process, the trader can buy and sell shares of high volume, paying only nominal margin money. Say by just paying Rupees 10000/-, the trader can buy/sell shares worth of Rupees 1 Lakh or more depending on the stockbroker.

- Short Term Trading –

  Herein the investor or trader buys and sells stocks in a short span of time, maybe a few days or few weeks or few months. In this process, the investor or trader buys shares at a specific price, hold it for some short period and sells when he or she gets the targeted price, and gets the desired profit. Herein the trader or the investor has to pay the full price of the shares at the time of buying.

- Long Term Investing –

  Herein the investor buys stocks to hold for a long period of time. In this process, the investor buys shares at a specific price, when he or she finds the buy price suitable, and then maybe hold it for years. In some cases, these investors buy the shares and never sell them during their lifetime, and then maybe pass on to the next generation as a part of the legacy. Herein also the investor has to pay the full price of the shares at the time of buying.

Steps to start investing in the equity market

- Decide how you want to invest in stocks.

- Open an investing account.

- Set a budget for your stock investment.

- Start investing or trading.

## Equity Mutual Funds

An equity fund is a mutual fund that invests principally in stocks. It can be actively or passively (index fund) managed. Equity funds are also known as stock funds. Stock mutual funds are principally categorized according to company size, the investment style of the holdings in the portfolio, and geography.

## Types of equity funds:

- Large Cap funds –

  These funds invest a large portion of their corpus in companies with large Market Capitalisation. These funds generally generate stable returns. Large-cap funds deliver steady returns with relatively lower risk, compared with midcap and small cap funds. They are ideal for investors with a lower risk appetite. With large cap funds, one needs to adopt a long-term perspective, stay patient, and remain invested to reap good returns over the long term.

- Mid Cap funds –

  These funds invest the maximum portion of their corpus in companies with market capitalisation lesser than large cap equities. During a bull phase, mid-cap stocks may outperform their large-cap counterparts, as these companies seek to expand by looking out for suitable growth opportunities. Investors should, however, note that the underlying stocks are more volatile than their large-cap counterparts. Mid Cap Funds are advised for investors who seek higher capital appreciation but have higher risk tolerance.

- Small cap funds –

These funds invest the maximum portion of their corpus in small cap equities, which refers to shares of companies with very less market capitalization. Smallcap funds typically outperform large-caps during a bull market but decline more when the sentiment turns bearish. Small cap funds are advised for investors who have a very high-risk tolerance.

- Sector Funds or Thematic Funds –

A sector fund or a thematic fund is a more specific and focused fund compared to a diversified equity mutual fund. For example, a sector fund will typically focus on just one particular industry group.

- Index Funds –

An index fund is a type of mutual fund with a portfolio constructed to match or track the components of a financial market index, such as the NIFTY or SENSEX. An index mutual fund follows its benchmark index irrespective of the state of the markets.

Legendary investor Warren Buffett has recommended index funds as a haven for savings for the sunset years of life. Rather than picking out individual stocks for investment, he has said, it makes more sense for the average investor to buy all of the S&P 500 companies at the low cost an index fund offers.

"Indexing" is a form of passive fund management. Instead of a fund portfolio manager doing active stock picking and market timing—that is, choosing securities to invest in and strategizing when to buy and sell them—the fund manager builds a portfolio whose holdings mirror the securities of a particular index. The idea is that by mimicking the profile of the index—the stock market as a whole, or a broad segment of it—the fund will match its performance as well.

- Equity Linked Savings Scheme (ELSS) –

An ELSS is an Equity Linked Savings Scheme, that allows an individual or HUF a deduction from the total income of up to Rupees 1.5 Lakhs under Section 80C of Income Tax Act 1961. Thus if an investor was to invest Rupees 50,000 in an ELSS, then this amount would be deducted from the total taxable income, thus reducing his or her tax burden.

The Long-Term Capital Gains (LTCG) on ELSS are tax-exempt up to Rupees 1 Lakh, and the dividend received is tax-free in the hands of investors. One can continue to invest or stay invested in this scheme even after the completion of the lock-in period of three years.

- Market capitalisation –

It refers to the value of a company that is traded on the stock market, which can be calculated by multiplying the total number of shares by the present share price.

- Short Term Capital Gains (STCG) –

The short-term capital gains (STCG) on the sale of listed equity shares and equity mutual funds are applicable when the holding period is less than one year from the date of purchase.

Short term capital gains are taxable at 15%, irrespective of tax slab. But, if total taxable income excluding short term gains is below taxable income i.e. Rupees 2.5 Lakhs, one can adjust this shortfall against short term gains.

- Long Term Capital Gains ((LTCG) –

The long-term capital gains (LTCG) on the sale of listed equity shares and equity mutual funds have been made taxable from 1 April 2018. In the case of equity investing, long-term means a holding period of more than one year from the date of purchase.

Long-term capital gains accrued from selling equity shares and equity-oriented mutual funds are exempt from tax for a maximum up to Rupees 1 Lakh in a financial year. The gains in excess of Rs 1 Lakh are chargeable at the rate of a flat 10 percent.

Thus, if nett LTCG (after setting off any eligible losses) from selling of equity shares and equity mutual funds in FY 2018-19 is Rupees 1.2 Lakh, then one will be required to pay tax only on Rs 20,000.

Budget 2018 proposed to remove Section 10 (38) of the Income Tax Act, 1961. As per this section, the long-term capital gains (LTCG) arising on the sale of equity shares or units of an equity-oriented mutual fund on which Securities Transaction Tax (STT) is paid was exempt from taxation. This section was initially introduced through the Finance Act, 2004, with effect from AY 2005-06, based on the Kelkar Committee report to attract investments from Foreign Institutional Investors (FII).

# CHAPTER 7

# Commodity

Commodities are also a very good form of Investment. It helps in creating long term wealth, only if someone is ready to take some risk and experience some volatility.

Commodities include gold, silver, crude oil, copper, nickel, lead, zinc, and many agri-commodities.

They can be bought directly from the open market. Or can be traded in the commodity exchanges.

Gold has been the most important commodity that people have perceived as the most favourite wealth making tool.

Crude oil is another most important commodity as it is supposed to be the barometer of the economy. When the global economy is growing, crude oil prices are expected to rise due to high demand. When the global economy is in recession, crude oil prices are expected to fall due to low demand.

In India, commodities can be traded through 2 leading exchanges, namely MCX (Multi commodity exchange) and

NCDEX (National commodity and derivative exchange). Both MCX and NCDEX are headquartered in Mumbai and came into operation in 2003.

## MCX trades in

- Bullion — gold and silver.

- Base Metals — aluminium, copper, nickel, lead, and zinc.

- Energy — crude oil and natural gas.

- Agro commodities — cardamom, cotton. crude palm oil, kapas, mentha oil.

## NCDEX trades in

- Cereals and Pulses - Barley, chana, maize kharif, maize, rabi, wheat, moong and paddy (basmati).

- Fibres—Kapas and 29 mm cotton.

- Guar complex— Guar seed and guar gum.

- Oil and oil seeds— castor seed, cotton seed oil cake, soybean, refined soy oil, mustard seed, and crude palm oil.

- Sugar.

Normally gold and silver have been seen as common wealth creation avenue. The rest of the commodities are just for trading profits. Indians have been known for ages for purchasing gold and silver items and preserving them for generations.

Historic prices of Gold can be seen as follows:

| Average Historic Price of 24 karat Gold per 10 grams | | | | | |
|---|---|---|---|---|---|
| Year | Price | Year | Price | Year | Price |
| 1964 | Rs. 63.25 | 1983 | Rs. 1,800.00 | 2002 | Rs. 4,990.00 |
| 1965 | Rs. 71.75 | 1984 | Rs. 1,970.00 | 2003 | Rs. 5,600.00 |
| 1966 | Rs. 83.75 | 1985 | Rs. 2,130.00 | 2004 | Rs. 5,850.00 |
| 1967 | Rs. 102.50 | 1986 | Rs. 2,140.00 | 2005 | Rs. 7,000.00 |
| 1968 | Rs. 162.00 | 1987 | Rs. 2,570.00 | 2006 | Rs. 8,400.00 |
| 1969 | Rs. 176.00 | 1988 | Rs. 3,130.00 | 2007 | Rs. 10,800.00 |
| 1970 | Rs. 184.00 | 1989 | Rs. 3,140.00 | 2008 | Rs. 12,500.00 |
| 1971 | Rs. 193.00 | 1990 | Rs. 3,200.00 | 2009 | Rs. 14,500.00 |
| 1972 | Rs. 202.00 | 1991 | Rs. 3,466.00 | 2010 | Rs. 18,500.00 |
| 1973 | Rs. 278.50 | 1992 | Rs. 4,334.00 | 2011 | Rs. 26,400.00 |
| 1974 | Rs. 506.00 | 1993 | Rs. 4,140.00 | 2012 | Rs. 31,050.00 |
| 1975 | Rs. 540.00 | 1994 | Rs. 4,598.00 | 2013 | Rs. 29,600.00 |
| 1976 | Rs. 432.00 | 1995 | Rs. 4,680.00 | 2014 | Rs. 28,006.50 |
| 1977 | Rs. 486.00 | 1996 | Rs. 5,160.00 | 2015 | Rs. 26,343.50 |
| 1978 | Rs. 685.00 | 1997 | Rs. 4,725.00 | 2016 | Rs. 28,623.50 |
| 1979 | Rs. 937.00 | 1998 | Rs. 4,045.00 | 2017 | Rs. 29,667.50 |
| 1980 | Rs. 1,330.00 | 1999 | Rs. 4,234.00 | 2018 | Rs. 31,438.00 |
| 1981 | Rs. 1,800.00 | 2000 | Rs. 4,400.00 | 2019 | Rs. 35,220.00 |
| 1982 | Rs. 1,645.00 | 2001 | Rs. 4,300.00 | 2020 | Rs. 50,000.00 |

Historic prices of Silver can be seen as follows:

| Historic Silver Rates in Rs./Kg. | | | |
|---|---|---|---|
| Date | Price | Date | Price |
| 31.03.1981 | 2,715 | 31.03.2002 | 7,875 |
| 31.03.1982 | 2,720 | 31.03.2003 | 7,695 |
| 31.03.1983 | 3,105 | 31.03.2004 | 11,770 |
| 31.03.1984 | 3,570 | 31.03.2005 | 10,675 |
| 31.03.1985 | 3,955 | 31.03.2006 | 17,405 |
| 31.03.1986 | 4,015 | 31.03.2007 | 19,520 |
| 31.03.1987 | 4,794 | 31.03.2008 | 23,625 |
| 31.03.1988 | 6,066 | 31.03.2009 | 22,165 |
| 31.03.1989 | 6,755 | 31.03.2010 | 27,255 |
| 31.03.1990 | 6,463 | 31.03.2011 | 56,900 |
| 31.03.1991 | 6,646 | 31.03.2012 | 56,290 |
| 31.03.1992 | 8,040 | 31.03.2013 | 54,030 |
| 31.03.1993 | 5,489 | 31.03.2014 | 43,070 |
| 31.03.1994 | 7,124 | 31.03.2015 | 37,825 |
| 31.03.1995 | 6,335 | 31.03.2016 | 36,990 |
| 31.03.1996 | 7,346 | 31.03.2017 | 38,058 |
| 31.03.1997 | 7,345 | 31.03.2018 | 38,355 |
| 31.03.1998 | 8,560 | 31.03.2019 | 37,245 |
| 31.03.1999 | 7,615 | 31.03.2020 | 33,867 |
| 31.03.2000 | 7,900 | 30.04.2020 | 41,520 |
| 31.03.2001 | 7,215 | 31.12.2020 | 68,000 |

Thus we can see the huge wealth creation of gold and silver.

Rupees 63.25 invested in gold in 1964 has become Rupees 50000 in 2020. That is 790 times growth in 56 years.

Rupees. 2715 invested in silver in 1981 has become Rupees 68000 in 2020. That is 25 times growth in 39 years.

So, gold and silver have been popular among Indians for wealth creation.

# CHAPTER 8

# Life Insurance

Life Insurance is the most important tool, that helps to create long term wealth and also a legacy for the next generations, though it has never been a very sought-after investment tool.

Life Insurance might not help to grow wealth many folds but can help in stable growth, and most importantly help to protect the financial wealth created, from any unfortunate mishap.

Currently in India, Life Insurance is of mainly 4 types:

- Term Insurance.

- Unit Linked Insurance Plans (ULIP).

- Conventional Insurance Plans with Guaranteed Bonus.

- Conventional Insurance Plans with Variable Bonus.

## Term Insurance

It gives high life coverage at a very nominal premium. But pure term insurance does not have any maturity value.

Term Plan mainly comes with two variants as below:

- Pure Term Insurance without Return of Premium Option
- Term Insurance with Return of Premium Option

## Example of Pure Term Insurance without Return of Premium

Say a 40-year aged man takes pure term insurance for Rupees 50 Lakhs sum assured for 30 years term, at Rupees 20000 annual premium. In case he dies within the 30 years term, his nominee gets Rupees 50 Lakhs. And in case he survives the 30 years term, he or his family gets nothing.

## Example of Term Insurance with Return of Premium

Say a 40-year aged man takes term insurance, with the return of premium option, for Rupees 50 Lakhs for 30 years term, at Rupees 30000 annual premium. In case he dies within the 30 years term, his nominee gets Rupees 50 Lakhs. And in case he survives the 30 years term, he gets the refund of Rupees 9 Lakh premium he paid, without any interest.

## Unit Linked Insurance Plan (ULIP)

It is an insurance plan, which offers a market-linked investment option along with life insurance coverage, under a single plan.

Say a 40-year aged man takes a unit-linked insurance plan of Rupees 5 Lakhs annual premium for 30 years policy term and ten years payment term. In that case, he would get a life coverage of Rupees 50 Lakhs. In case he dies within the 30 years term, his nominee gets Rupees 50 Lakhs. And in case he survives the 30 years term, he gets back the total fund value, created out of his investment of Rupees 50 Lakhs, paid in a span of 10 years. He might also withdraw the total fund value after completion of 5 years, closing the policy. In that case, the life coverage also ceases as soon as the policy is closed.

A unit-linked insurance plan gives a good return if the stock market performance is good during the investment period. And the returns are not good if the stock market performance is not good during the investment period.

Returns from unit linked insurance plans are 100% tax-free under section 10 (10D).

## Conventional Insurance Plans with Guaranteed Bonus

It is an insurance plan which gives guaranteed life coverage along-with a guaranteed maturity value, which includes a guaranteed sum assured plus a guaranteed bonus, after a stipulated policy term.

For example: say a policy holder is expected to pay Rupees 1 Lakh annually for 10 years and is supposed to get back guaranteed Rupees 25 Lakhs after 20 years, wherein Rupees 10 Lakhs is sum assured and Rupees 15 Lakhs is guaranteed bonus.

These types of plans are better than bank fixed deposits as the returns are tax-free under section 10(10D) of the income tax act, and the returns are guaranteed. The rate of interest gets fixed at the time of taking the policy. Even if the bank rate of interest decreases with time, the returns from this policy will remain the same throughout the total policy term of 20 years, and the rate of return will stay constant for all the 10 annual premiums.

## Conventional Insurance Plans with Variable Bonus

It is an insurance plan which gives guaranteed life coverage along-with a non-guaranteed maturity value, which includes a guaranteed sum assured plus variable bonus, after a stipulated policy term.

For example: say a policy holder is expected to pay Rupees 1 Lakh annually for 10 years and is supposed to get back Rupees 10 Lakhs sum assured and accrued bonus as declared every year.

Originally all non-market linked life insurance policies were like these, before the introduction of 100% guaranteed plans. With a falling bank rate of interest, bonus rates have got reduced. In the 1990s, the bank rate of interest was around 12% per annum, and the bonus rate on life insurance policies was around Rupees 70 per thousand, calculated on the sum assured every year. Currently, the bank rate of interest is around 6% per annum, and the bonus rate on life insurance policies are around Rupees 40 per thousand, calculated on the sum assured every year. In the coming years, the bank rate of interest and bonus rate on life insurance might keep falling. So if there is an option, in the current Indian market scenario, it is best to take policies with guaranteed bonuses.

To get pure protection or life coverage, one should buy term insurance.

To get life coverage along with market-linked returns, one should buy a unit-linked insurance plan.

To get life coverage along with guaranteed returns, one should buy conventional insurance plans with guaranteed bonus.

And at any cost, one should avoid buying conventional insurance plans with variable bonus, if conventional insurance plans with guaranteed bonus are available.

# CHAPTER 9

# Health Insurance

Health insurance is not a direct investment tool. But it can help in the creation of wealth. It results in huge savings, in case there is any medical emergency in the family. Say if someone is hospitalised in a family, and it results in a hefty hospital bill of Rupees 10 Lakhs. Now, if there is health insurance of sum assured of more than Rupees 10 Lakhs, the entire bill gets paid by the health insurance company. Otherwise, Rupees 10 Lakhs has to be liquidated from savings.

Say one pays a hospital bill of Rupees 10 Lakhs at the age of 40 from his savings, he ends up losing Rupees 10 Lakhs plus its time value. At the age of 60, that Rupees 10 Lakhs might have become Rupees 40 Lakhs. Thus paying a small annual premium towards health insurance, might end up in huge savings, thereby help in creating huge wealth.

Currently, health insurances available in India can be broadly divided into 3 types:

1. Individual Policy

2. Family Floater Policy

3. Top Up Policy

An individual mediclaim policy is a type of health cover where a single person is covered under a single plan. The premium rate of such a plan is decided after assessing the age, health and lifestyle conditions of the proposer.

Say in a family of two, husband and wife, two individual mediclaim policies are taken, in the name of the two individuals, of Rupees 3 Lakhs each. In that case, each person can claim up to Rupees 3 Lakhs only.

A family floater covers all the family members under one single plan. The sum insured is fixed and gets exhausted as and when any member avails medical services and makes a claim. The members coverable under a family floater can be the policyholder and his/her parents, spouse, and children.

Say in a family of two, husband and wife, one family floater mediclaim policy is taken, jointly in the name of the two individuals, of Rupees 6 Lakhs total. In that case, any person can claim upto Rs. 6 Lakhs only, or two people can claim up to Rupees 6 Lakhs combined.

A top-up plan supplements a base health insurance plan by providing additional coverage above the sum assured available on the base plan. In the case of a top-up plan, there is a deductible amount, which is nothing but the initial claim amount that is not covered under the policy. The claim amounts that cross the deductible amount, is paid under a top-up plan.

Say a family takes a top-up plan of Rupees 15 Lakhs, with Rupees 3 Lakhs as deductible, any hospital bill exceeding Rupees 3 Lakhs will be paid, after deducting Rupees 3 Lakhs, as it is supposed to be claimed through the base policy.

Thus, it is important for everyone to have a mediclaim policy, be it, individual policy, or family floater policy.

# CHAPTER 10

# Real Estate

Real Estate has been one of the most trusted option for wealth creation for ages, both in India and worldwide.

The major mindset was to buy properties, be it land or ready property, and hold it for a long period, and then sell it after a good price appreciation. There was a strong belief, that real estate prices will be always appreciating.

The common practise had been, if someone had an investable surplus, he or she would purchase a plot of land or a ready flat, and hold it for 7-10 Years, and then sell it off, after the price had appreciated.

If interest rates are at record lows, it may be a good time to buy, as you will pay a reduced cost for the privilege of borrowing money. If property values are on the decline, it may be a good time to wait as you could end up getting a better deal on the same type of home in just a few months.

How do you create wealth in real estate?

- Buy real estate in upcoming neighbourhoods.

- Know your 'why' before investing.

- Do proper research before investing.

- Rent out residential real estate, if possible.

There are many ways to build wealth, but real estate used to be considered the safest, steadiest, and simplest way of wealth creation.

But real estate also has certain disadvantages. It includes very high transaction costs, as each time a sale takes place, the government has to be given a large sum of money, in form of registration fees. Also, there are costs such as legal fees, brokerage, renovation and maintenance costs which are involved in every real estate transaction.

# CHAPTER 11

# Smart Step 1: Do proper Financial Planning and Goal Setting

One should do proper financial planning and goal setting, before deciding on any new investment. One should set financial goals after proper need analysis. Say, before deciding when and where to invest for children's future or retirement, one needs to decide how much amount is required for children's future or retirement, and that too after how many years. So one needs to first decide on his or her requirements, before planning any investment.

Common Steps of Financial Planning:

1. Need analysis.

2. Financial goal setting.

3. Planning asset allocation.

4.  Planning portfolio diversification.

5.  Reviewing existing investments.

6.  Analysing protection needs.

7.  Planning protection portfolio.

8.  Planning investment portfolio.

# CHAPTER 12

# Smart Step 2: Maintain Necessary Liquidity

One should have the necessary liquidity in hand. Life sometimes presents a lot of uncertainties that require immediate cash. So if there are sufficient funds in a savings account or liquid fixed deposits or liquid funds, one does not need to liquidate equity investments or take a loan.

Equity funds need to be liquidated when equity valuations are high. At the time of emergency, if there is no liquidity in debt investments or cash, one might have to liquidate equity investments, even if it results in losses, which is not at all advisable. So it is always advised to have sufficient liquidity in form of cash or liquid funds, to overcome any sort of crisis.

Having sufficient liquidity at the time of any emergency also helps psychologically. As the liquid cash helps to overcome the crisis easily. It is a prescribed practice to maintain 3-6 months of expenses as an emergency liquidity fund.

# CHAPTER 13

# Smart Step 3: Have Proper Risk Coverage

Having sufficient risk coverage does not help in growing wealth. But not having sufficient risk coverage, can result in loss of wealth, in case of any unfortunate incident.

If the sole earning member dies in a road accident, without sufficient life insurance, it can lead to huge wealth loss for the family. If any Family member gets hospitalised due to some critical disease, and there is no health insurance, it can lead to huge wealth loss for the family.

So, it always advisable to have sufficient risk coverage, in form of life insurance and health insurance.

Ideally, life insurance cover should be 15 to 20 times of annual income. Industry experts often recommend this simple formula. For example - If one's annual income is Rs.6 lakh, then one should have a life insurance cover for a minimum of Rs. 90 lakh to Rs.1.20 crore.

There is no fixed rule for how much health insurance one needs.

One can have health insurance cover of Rupees 5 Lakhs for people earning up to Rupees 2.5 Lakhs,Rupees 10 Lakhs for people earning up to Rupees 5 Lakhs, and Rupees 20 Lakhs for people earning Rupees 10 Lakhs and above.

Also, people living in Tier 1 cities can have a health cover of at least Rupees 10 Lakhs because treatment costs in such cities are high. For those staying in Tier 2 and Tier 3 cities, the health insurance cover may be of Rupees 5 Lakhs.

Also one should always choose a family floater health insurance cover.

# CHAPTER 14

# Smart Step 4: Plan for Long Term

Always one should plan for the long term and not the short term. Priority should always be towards creating long term value rather than creating short term profit.

For example: one shouldn't look for stocks that grow from Rupees 100 to Rupees 120 in maybe one year but look for stocks which can grow from Rupees 100 to Rupees 1000 in maybe ten years' time horizon.

Real wealth can be created only with long term vision. Short term vision can help one buy Gold at Rupees 22000 (Per 10 Gms) and sell at Rupees 25000 (Per 10 Gms). Long term vision can help one buy Gold at Rupees 22000 (Per 10 Gms) and hold till Rupees 47000 (Per 10 Gms).

So, one should always have a long-term vision.

# CHAPTER 15

# Smart Step 5: Don't follow Past Performance Track blindly

---

Don't Invest as per past track, that is, don't invest in plans or commodities which have given extra-ordinary returns in the past.

Invest in plans or commodities, which might have given nominal or negative returns in the recent past, but has a huge potential in the coming future.

So, the best strategy is to buy when everyone is selling, and sell when everyone is buying.

Say gold has appreciated from Rupees 30000 (Per 10 Gms) to Rupees 47000 (Per 10 Gms) in past one year. It might not be wise to invest in gold looking at the past performance.

Now say Silver has appreciated from Rupees 37000 (Per Kilogram) to Rupees 47000 (Per Per Kilogram) in past four years. Now, if there is the scope of appreciation of silver prices in the coming days, even if past performance has not been very good, it might be wise to invest in silver not giving much importance to the past performance.

# CHAPTER 16

# Smart Step 6: Don't follow others blindly

One should not copy others or listen to tips or rumours. One should either do self-research before investing or consult some good adviser.

Say Mr. Rakesh Jhunjhunwala has invested in Delta Corp. He might have done so based on a specific study, with some specific entry and exit strategy. So just following him blindly and investing in Delta Corp might not help.

Say CNBC TV18 is telling that Silver will become Rupees 1 Lakh (Per Kilogram) very shortly. So following CNBC TV18 and holding on to the investments of Silver, and not booking profits at Rupees 72000 (Per Kilogram), might turn out to be a very foolish decision.

One should always do certain research before doing any investments. Nowadays all information has become easily accessible over the internet. So doing self-research regarding any financial product or commodity has become very easy.

So it is always advisable to do certain self-research before investing.

Also one can consult some good financial adviser before investing. As every work is specialised, a good financial adviser can give better advice regarding investments.

# Smart Step 7: Always review the portfolio periodically

This is the most important strategy. One should always keep reviewing and restructuring existing investments regularly, as market conditions keep changing.

One should exit from investment plans/schemes giving low or negative returns.

And one should increase investment amount in investment plans/schemes giving good returns.

Also one needs to maintain proper investment diversification. "One should never put all eggs in a single basket".

Ideally, the investment portfolio should be reviewed every six months or one year. It helps to book profit on time. Also, it saves one from a bigger loss that can accrue in a single scheme, over a longer time horizon.

# CHAPTER 18

# Common Mistakes that common investors should avoid

1.  **No proper financial goal setting and need analysis.**

    People normally try to decide on investment products, by seeing advertisements and recommendations from friends, without deciding on financial goals and individual needs. It needs to be understood that financial needs and product suitability varies from person to person.

2.  **Going by Herd Mentality. Following other Investors. Listening to Market Pundits.**

    People normally try to follow others for investment decisions. One needs to understand everyone's financial objectives in life cannot be identical. Also listening to various pundits blindly, without doing any self-research can be suicidal.

### 3. Chasing past profits

People normally invest seeing the past track. Say if the share of State Bank of India moved up from Rupees 150 to Rupees 250 in the past 6 months, people tend to buy shares of State Bank of India at Rupees 250, expecting it to move to Rupees 350 within the next 6 months. At Rupees 150 it didn't look attractive for investment, but at Rupees 250 it looks attractive for investment. This is the biggest blunder that common investors make.

### 4. Becoming risk-averse due to current losses

People normally enter the bull markets when all prices are rising. And exit in losses in bear markets when all prices are falling. And then vow never to invest in stock markets.

### 5. Having short term vision

People look for short term gains, which are not possible. People look to double their money in maybe 6 months/1 year, which might not be practically feasible. And this greed leads to losses.

### 6. Booking profits early

Say a share moved up from Rupees 100 to Rupees 200. But maximum investors might not have the patience to hold for longer, but maybe sell-off after taking Rupees 10 – Rupees 20 Profit. Though there are booked profit, we can say there is a notional loss. And these small profits do not help in wealth creation.

7.   **Holding on to loss for long**

Say a share moved down from Rupees 200 to Rupees 100. But maximum investors might not exit at Rupees 10 – Rupees 20 loss but hold on to the losses for longer. Though there is no booked loss, we can say there is a huge notional loss. And these huge losses erode wealth, as at some point in time, losses will be booked.

8.   **Ignoring market trends**

People tend to invest or average out when stock prices start falling. It is like trying to catch a falling knife. Say an investor has invested in stock at Rupees 100. And the stock price has started falling. The investor keeps averaging on every fall of Rupees 10. This is a good strategy if the Price recovers fast after a fall of Rupees 20 – Rupees 30. But it may always not be so. If the stock price moves to Rupees 50, the investor ends up adding a huge volume of the stock. Though the average cost price might have come down, the net loss might have increased manifold. So this is one of the big mistakes that a common investor makes.

9. **Not doing proper self-research**

   When we buy a mobile phone of Rupees 10000, we do a lot of research. But while investing Rupees 100000, we don't do even 1/10th of that research. This is a very wrong approach.

10. **Not consulting good financial advisers**

    Like we should consult a doctor before taking any medicine, should we not consult a good and proficient financial adviser before deciding on any investment. Maximum investors don't feel the need to consult a good financial adviser. This is also a very wrong approach.

# Conclusion

Indian financial markets have still not matured. Indian clients are also not very aware of the various investment opportunities available in the Indian financial markets. And financial advisors tend not to brief the clients about the various risk factors.

The objective of this book is to educate the readers and clients about various investment opportunities and probable financial goals, so that they can take all future financial decisions, wisely and prudently.

I hope after reading this book, clients will not have to depend blindly on financial advisers or news-channels or news-magazines.

I hope I have been able to progress to a certain extent in my mission. But my mission and efforts to educate the investor community will continue.

## NOTES:

**NOTES:**

**NOTES:**

**NOTES:**

www.ingramcontent.com/pod-product-compliance
Lightning Source LLC
Chambersburg PA
CBHW051802130726

47987CB00003B/1076